J. COLE

CHART-TOPPING RAPPER

BY ALICIA Z. KLEPEIS

Essential Library

An Imprint of Abdo Publishing
abdopublishing.com

ABDOPUBLISHING.COM

Published by Abdo Publishing, a division of ABDO, PO Box 398166, Minneapolis, Minnesota 55439. Copyright © 2018 by Abdo Consulting Group, Inc. International copyrights reserved in all countries. No part of this book may be reproduced in any form without written permission from the publisher. Essential Library™ is a trademark and logo of Abdo Publishing.

Printed in the United States of America, North Mankato, Minnesota
102017
012018

**THIS BOOK CONTAINS
RECYCLED MATERIALS**

Cover Photo: Scott Roth/Invision/AP Images
Interior Photos: Tim Mosenfelder/Getty Images Entertainment/Getty Images, 4, 10–11; Joe Seer/Shutterstock Images, 14, 51; Seth Poppel/Yearbook Library, 18; Jack Arent/National Basketball Association/Getty Images, 22; Debby Wong/Shutterstock Images, 28–29, 39, 68; Mark Allen/AP Images, 32–33; Shutterstock Images, 40–41; Chris Pizzello/Invision/AP Images, 42; Marcin Kadziolka/Shutterstock Images, 45; Frank Micelotta/Invision/AP Images, 47; Scott Roth/Invision/AP Images, 48–49, 84–85; Raymond Boyd/Michael Ochs Archives/Getty Images, 54; A. Katz/Shutterstock Images, 56–57; Theo Wargo/WireImage/Getty Images, 61; Denis Linine/Shutterstock Images, 67; Johnny Nunez/WireImage/Getty Images, 70–71, 92–93; Angela Weiss/AFP/Getty Images, 74–75; Taylor Hill/Getty Images Entertainment/Getty Images, 76–77; Gallo Images/Getty Images, 80–81; Sterling Munksgard/Shutterstock Images, 86–87; Matt Rourke/Getty Images, 94–95; Nicholas Hunt/Getty Images Entertainment/Getty Images, 96

Editor: Brenda Haugen
Series Designer: Laura Polzin

PUBLISHER'S CATALOGING-IN-PUBLICATION DATA

Names: Klepeis, Alicia Z., author.
Title: J. Cole: chart-topping rapper / by Alicia Z. Klepeis.
Other titles: Chart-topping rapper
Description: Minneapolis, Minnesota : Abdo Publishing, 2018. | Series: Hip-hop artists | Includes online resources and index.
Identifiers: LCCN 2017946868 | ISBN 9781532113260 (lib.bdg.) | ISBN 9781532152146 (ebook)
Subjects: LCSH: Cole, J., (Jermaine), 1985-.--Juvenile literature. | Rap musicians--United States--Biography--Juvenile literature. | Rap (Music)--Juvenile literature.
Classification: DDC 782.421649 [B]--dc23
LC record available at https://lccn.loc.gov/2017946868

CONTENTS

A SOLD-OUT SHOW

N ew York City's Madison Square Garden was sold out on August 4, 2015, and the crowd was cheering so loudly it was almost deafening. As J. Cole performed his track "Nobody's Perfect," he kept the crowd of 13,665 people excited. He invited the throng of fans to join in: "New York City, sing this!"[1]

Cole's shadow loomed large in the round spotlight behind him. Long, bright blue and yellow beams of light streamed all the way from the base of the stage to up high into the rafters. Fog along the edge of the stage gave a misty, atmospheric feel to the space.

Throughout the show, the crowd stayed engaged. People jumped up and down, waved their arms in the air, and sang or rapped along as Cole performed tunes from his album *2014 Forest Hills Drive*. Sometimes Cole stood by his mic and did call-and-response with the

Parts of the Forest Hills Drive tour set looked like a neighborhood.

audience. At other times, he moved quickly from one side of the stage to the other. A huge video projection screen live-streamed the performance so everyone in the arena, even the fans way up in the stands, could see him clearly. The lights were dazzling and varied from one moment to the next. Red, white, and blue spotlights brightened the scene briefly. Minutes later, flower-shaped light projections flickered on the stage floor.

AN INCREDIBLE SET

The set of Cole's Forest Hills Drive tour provided an amazing part of the concert experience for fans. The set was specially designed to fit with the tour's featured album. The floor of the stage looked like the side of a house. It was covered in siding and had several windows punctuating the house's facade. The house was crucial to Cole's *2014 Forest Hills Drive* album as well as the performer's life story. As Cole's production manager and audio engineer Ray Rogers noted, "This tour is really all about him growing up and the impact of that house."[2] A Forest Hills Drive street sign and bright red stop sign stood on the stage, adding more realistic details to the set.

At various points during the show, high-powered flare strobe lights shone up through the house's windows.

The lights flickered on and off and changed color as Cole performed. The high-tech set also provided the illusion of looking up into the sky while lying between two houses, thanks to trees and moving clouds projected on a large screen.

"This is a great looking and sounding tour, very theatrical with a big visceral impact."[4]

– Craig Mitchell, LMG touring company's director of touring

SHARING HIS MESSAGE

Throughout the show, Cole took time out from rapping to talk candidly with his fans. As *Vibe* magazine writer Adelle Platon noted, "In front of a sold-out crowd at Madison Square Garden on Tuesday night (Aug.4), J. Cole is treating the stage as his personal stoop."[3]

At one point, Cole spoke about how people worship celebrities and their fame and possessions. And yet, at that very moment, Cole's

SAINT TROPEZ

During the Madison Square Garden concert, Cole talked about Saint Tropez and how he would not be able to find it on a map even if he were paid a million dollars. Cole mentions this hot spot on the French Riviera in his song "St. Tropez," and he told his New York audience he would like to see it someday. Saint Tropez has been used in the hip-hop genre as a metaphor for fortune and fame. For example, in his song "I Get Money," 50 Cent raps: "I did play the block, now I play on boats / In the south of France baby, Saint Tropez."[5]

appearance was vastly different from many other rappers. Sitting on the floor of the stage, he was dressed simply in a black T-shirt, long black shorts, and a pair of work boots. He wore no flashy designer attire nor any serious bling.

Cole explained to the audience the meaning behind his album *2014 Forest Hills Drive*. He said the world is constantly bombarding people with images of what is supposed to make them happy. Cole explained that the American dream always includes having a lot of money, a big house, a big car, and a spouse who looks perfect. Cole said those things are not what it takes to be happy. He asked the audience what people need to be happy and was delighted when the audience responded with his desired answer—love.

At another point in the show, the 30-year-old artist talked about his own experiences growing up in the small city of Fayetteville, North Carolina. He said a lot

Cole on the set of his Forest Hills Drive tour

of times people suffer from what he called a "small-town mentality."[6] He mentioned that when little kids growing up in small towns see cities such as Los Angeles, New

York City, Paris, or London in the media, they tell
themselves that when they get older, they will go there.
As those children grow older, they become afraid to go to

big cities or other places to explore. Cole shared his own story about leaving Fayetteville: "I took a leap of faith and I moved." He told the audience that he headed to New York to work on his music and never stopped. He shared some of his own failures and disappointments from his journey.

But Cole also shared some overarching messages, including to never "stop believing in yourself."[7]

NATURAL BEAUTY

Some of Cole's songs touch on the importance people place on beauty and the products people feel they should use, from fake nails and hair weaves to makeup. Cole's song "Crooked Smile" also mentions his own thick eyebrows and twisted "grill," or teeth, but says, "We ain't picture perfect but we worth the picture still." The lyrics go on to tell women to love themselves and embrace their natural beauty: "No need to fix what God already put his paintbrush on."[9]

LOTS OF LOVE

Later in the show, thousands of cell phone flashlights illuminated the darkness of the huge arena. Cole sat on the stage's floor and started singing an iconic line from his wildly popular song "Love Yourz": "No such thing as a life that's better than yours / No such thing as a life that's better than yours."[8] The voices of the audience chimed in, repeating the lines of this powerful hook over and over again.

Dozens of bright white spotlights lined the stage's edge, lighting it up. Close behind Cole, a clear, steady drumbeat sounded. Throughout the song, Cole raised his hands in the air, pointed at himself, and even imitated someone using a TV remote. "Love Yourz" was the last song of the concert. When Cole finished singing it, he stood up and signed off by saying, "Peace and love."[10] Another wildly successful concert by Jermaine Cole had reached its conclusion.

FROM DAYDREAMS TO REALITY

Cole had visions of playing at Madison Square Garden before it actually happened. He told a reporter that he was either riding his bike or walking past the venue and thought to himself, "One day I'ma do that."[11] Just three months later, Cole sold out the arena in just one day. "It's crazy. So ridiculous. It's insane," Cole mused.[12] His August 4 show at the Garden earned $1 million in ticket sales, his biggest take of the summer.[13]

FINDING HIS MUSIC

Jermaine Lamarr Cole was born on January 28, 1985, on a US army base in Frankfurt, which was part of West Germany at the time. His older brother, Zach, was a toddler when Jermaine arrived. Jermaine's father was an African-American soldier. His mother, Kay, was white.

Jermaine's parents split up when he was still a baby. When Jermaine was just eight months old, Kay moved with him and his brother to Fayetteville, North Carolina. Kay struggled financially, taking a number of jobs over the years.

During his early childhood, Jermaine lived in trailer parks with his mom and brother. In a 2011 National Public Radio interview, he talked about one of the trailer parks in which they lived: "It was one of the scariest places I've been to, because I was always worried about my mother."[1] Eventually, Kay married another military man.

Growing up, Jermaine's life was far from the world of the designer parties and award ceremonies he would attend as an adult.

COMPETITIVE STREAK

Jermaine admits that he has been competitive since he was a little kid. When he was in the first grade, he went up to his teacher's desk and asked her what his grade average was. Jermaine later recalled the teacher's reaction: "'Man, you're in the first grade! Why do you want your average?'"[2] But Jermaine saw it as a competition. He wanted to have the best grades in his class. The drive to do things well has remained with him to this day.

"We had this condescending stepfather figure who was really negative. There was no love, no connection there. He was physically abusive to us and verbally abusive too, even more so to my brother."[3]

– *J. Cole*

Unfortunately, the new man in Kay's life was not a source of positive energy in the household.

NEW HOUSE, NEW LIFE?

Jermaine's stepdad was not the supportive father figure the elementary-school-aged boy might have wanted. But there was one big change for the better in Jermaine's life. In 1996, when he was 11 years old, his family moved to a nicer house near a creek on Forest Hills Drive. Jermaine lived there until he was 18.

Jermaine saw the new house as a kind of sanctuary. Years later, he said the home on Forest

Hills Drive had a huge impact on his life. In particular, having his own room was very important to his development. He valued having his own space to daydream, write, listen to music, and practice his raps in front of the mirror. He said that he became more reflective in his precious bedroom and that this space helped him turn into the person he became.

Jermaine loved his new space, but his life was far from perfect. He later recalled, "There were days when my mom would have to scrape up nickels and dimes to give me $1.50 lunch money. And I would know she wasn't eating lunch that day so that I could. . . . I was very aware that we were barely here [in the new house on Forest Hills Drive]."[4]

> "This is where I started dreaming the dream. . . . This room gave me the audacity to go to New York City to chase this dream."[5]
>
> – J. Cole

JERMAINE THE KANGAROO

Jermaine worked at other jobs before hitting the big time as a rapper. From the time he was 14 until he was 19, Jermaine was employed at a Fayetteville skating rink. He said it was "the best job" and called himself "the roll, bounce king."[6] On Saturdays and Sundays when little kids celebrated their birthdays, Jermaine dressed up as the mascot of the skating rink—a kangaroo.

A BUDDING RAPPER

Jermaine showed a passion for music even as a youth. In high school, he joined his school's orchestra as a violin player. He was the first-chair violinist, which meant he was one of the better musicians. In the orchestra, Jermaine performed tunes such as the theme songs from "Mission Impossible" and "Batman."

Jermaine as a freshman in high school

In addition to his orchestral musical experiences, Jermaine got involved with other types of music. He began rapping in 1997, at the age of 12, after seeing a cousin from Louisiana rap. In this early phase, Jermaine used rhyming words such as "soulja" and "doja."[7] He based his flow on hip-hop artist Master P.

When Jermaine was 12 or 13, he listened to rap lyrics that included swearing, and the rappers sang about smoking drugs. But Jermaine did not smoke anything. He moved on to create raps he described as battle raps, where he proved he could rap better than others.

His path to rap continued to progress as he got older. When he turned 15, he started telling stories in his songs. He chose to use his own life experiences to create songs that were more meaningful to him than battle raps. Instead of just bragging through battle raps,

UNDERSTANDING DIFFERENT PERSPECTIVES

Ever since he was a teenager, Jermaine liked to tell stories from real life. One of the factors that has influenced his writing is being biracial. In a 2011 interview with National Public Radio, he talked about his heritage: "I'm half-black, half-white, so I basically put it like this: I can fit in anywhere. That's why I write so many stories from so many different perspectives, because I've seen so many."[8]

MAKING CONNECTIONS

When Jermaine was a teen, the Internet was relatively new. At the time, he was a big fan of the rapper Canibus and participated in Canibus forums online. Through the forums, Jermaine connected with music producer Elite. Years later, Jermaine would work with Elite on his own music. Jermaine gave credit to Canibus's first album for influencing his approach to songwriting and for altering his own perspective on rap music.

he revealed more of himself in his music. Jermaine first rapped under the name Blaza and later as Therapist. Sometimes he got the idea for a rap name by looking through the dictionary.

BEAT MACHINES AND BOMM SHELTUH

Another important element in the development of Jermaine's early musical career involved the local rap duo Bomm Sheltuh, which included members FilthE Ritch and Nervous Reck. Jermaine got to know this group while he was a student at Terry Sanford High School, but it took some effort to get their attention. The group was putting on a show at Skate Zone, a local skating rink. There was a small part of the show when Bomm Sheltuh would allow people from the crowd to come up and rhyme. Despite his squeaky voice, 14-year-old Jermaine bravely performed in front of lots of older people. And in his own words, he "murdered."[9] After Jermaine's successful rhyming, Bomm Sheltuh let him come to their studio.

Once he had seen all the cool equipment at Bomm Sheltuh's studio, Jermaine wanted to produce his own music. For a year and a half, Jermaine begged his mom to get a beat machine. But the machines were expensive. Eventually, Kay gave 15-year-old Jermaine a $1,300 ASR-X for Christmas. As *Complex* reports, in exchange for the beat machine, Jermaine "agreed to buy his own clothes for the next year, skip out on getting a birthday present, and had to pay his own way to basketball camp the next summer."[10] He was thrilled with the new machine. It allowed him to start making his own beats and continue working on his own songs. So in addition to improving his rapping skills, Jermaine also started teaching himself to produce music. Jermaine stayed in touch with the members of Bomm Sheltuh for years after high school. They mentored Jermaine, helping him improve as a musician.

COLLEGE DAYS AND MIXTAPES

Jermaine Cole graduated from Terry Sanford High School in Fayetteville in 2003. After graduation, his next stop was New York City, where he attended Saint John's University in Queens on an academic scholarship. Cole chose to go to college in New York because that was where the rap scene was most active.

In college, Cole majored in communication and minored in business. He also was active in student life on campus. He might have made it onto the Saint John's men's basketball team as a walk-on, but he did not attend callbacks. He decided basketball was not what he wanted to do for the rest of his college career: "I decided that basketball was a pipe dream. It wasn't what I wanted to spend my next three or four years chasing. And that music was absolutely what I wanted to do."[1]

Cole still enjoys basketball, taking part in a celebrity basketball game in 2012.

During his senior year, he served as president of Haraya, the pan-African student coalition. This group, referred to as "the Black Student Union of Saint John's University," did community service and organized social events on campus. Haraya also set up events to educate the community about topics that interested its members.

Cole proved to be an excellent student. He graduated magna cum laude, or "with great honor," with a 3.8 grade-point average. Later he rapped about his grades on the track "Villuminati": "Couple more A's I would have been a Summa Cum Laude [with highest honor]."[2]

HIDDEN TALENTS

While Cole showed he was gifted in the classroom, not many people at Saint John's knew of his other talents.

During his college days, Cole stayed pretty quiet and did not share his dreams of being a rapper right away when meeting people. He later said, "Everyone was mad surprised that I rap. . . . I didn't broadcast it and go around with a rapper personality. I'm just Jermaine, walking around campus, making friends, and living my life."[4]

Cole worked hard in school by day, and at night he would toil away at whatever open mic nights or crowded nightclubs would have him. His persona was unlike many emcees who were flashy and full of themselves. As *Village Voice* writer Sowmya Krishnamurthy noted, "He was different . . . strangely normal and—gasp—approachable."[5] Despite his guy-next-door personality, Cole's talent and love for rap eventually got

A PARTY WITH THE STARS

In 2006, one of Cole's friends worked as an intern at Def Jam, an American record label mainly focused on hip-hop and urban music. She invited Cole to the 40/40 Club to celebrate Aaron Reid's sixteenth birthday. But this was not a proper invitation to the party. Instead, Cole's friend suggested he crash the party. Aaron is the son of songwriter and music producer Antonio "L.A." Reid. While Cole was not interested in going to a sixteenth birthday party, he decided to attend when he heard that Jay-Z, Swizz Beatz, and Kanye West would be there. Jay-Z walked past Cole but never noticed him. And by the time Cole realized it was Jay-Z walking by, it was too late to catch his attention.

people's attention. When he was a senior, he performed at open mic night at Carnesecca Arena on the Saint John's campus. The performance gave Cole some local exposure and showed his classmates and peers that a talented rapper was in their midst.

One person at Saint John's who really recognized Cole's musical talents was Ibrahim Hamad. He and Cole met while playing pickup basketball. One night Hamad and Cole were listening to music in a car on their way to a club in the city. Hamad heard a freestyle rap that he thought was awesome. When he asked Cole whose music they were listening to, Cole said it was his. Hamad was blown away by his friend's rapping skills. So even though they were both still students at Saint John's, Hamad made it his goal to start getting the word out about Cole's music. He started first in the New York City borough of Queens, contacting anyone he could think of who might be able to help kick-start Cole's career.

ODD JOBS AND MAKING MIXTAPES

Cole graduated with honors from Saint John's University in May 2007. After college, he tried to get a record deal. In the meantime, he needed money. He worked as a bill collector and as an ad salesman at a newspaper. He was not very good at either job and was barely scraping by. He still dreamed of making it as a rapper.

Cole changed his rap name from Therapist to J. Cole and then released his debut mixtape, *The Come Up*, on May 4, 2007. *The Come Up* was mostly self-produced. When an artist such as Cole self-produces a mixtape, he basically is in charge of all the stages of making the tape, including recording and mixing. Producers may also write material and select songs or other musicians to collaborate on a project. On the mixtape, Cole rapped over beats by several other rappers, including Just Blaze, Large Professor, and Kanye West. *The Come Up* generated some buzz and received positive reviews from the majority of those who heard it.

"I think *The Come Up* was . . . raw just straight rappin'. I am just trying to prove I can really rap with anybody."[6]

— *J. Cole*

CHASING HIS DREAM—AND JAY-Z

Cole wanted his music to be heard. So, when he finished his first mixtape, Cole set his sights high. He wanted to share his music with rap icon Jay-Z. There are a number of versions of the story of their first meeting. According to the version of events from a National Public Radio

interview, Cole camped for hours outside of the music studio where Jay-Z worked. When Jay-Z walked by, Cole stuck out his hand to offer the CD to him. But Jay-Z did not accept Cole's offering, which was devastating for the young artist.

But Cole has never been a quitter. The negative experience with Jay-Z did not make Cole give up. In 2007, Cole signed with the Sony/Jive record label. Mark Pitts, who served as president of urban music at Sony/Jive, spoke highly of Cole: "J. Cole personifies humility and grace with edge and depth. As an MC, his point of view speaks to and represents me. I'm proud and blessed to be a part of his journey!"[7]

ROC NATION AND MORE MIXTAPES

Cole continued to work on his music. He released his next mixtape, *The Warm Up*, on June 15, 2009. Cole said the mixtape looked back on the previous five years of his life. He also hoped it would inspire others who

J. COLE BECOMES AN *XXL* FRESHMAN

Cole's face was seen in newsstands across the country on March 16, 2010. He was featured in *XXL* magazine's annual Freshman tribute to up-and-coming artists in hip-hop, also known as the 2010 Hip-Hop Preview. Cole was featured on the cover with several musicians, including Pill, Wiz Khalifa, and Big Sean. Some music industry insiders wondered if perhaps Cole was "too normal" and might be easily forgotten in the rap world of larger-than-life stars.[9] When Cole heard these concerns, he initially wondered if he needed to change his image but quickly decided to stay true to himself.

might be pursuing their own dreams.

In a letter Cole wrote on the five-year anniversary of this mixtape, he said, "*The Warm Up* is a declaration of dedication to Greatness. Told from the perspective of a kid who wants more than what his city has to offer him. The crime. The stagnation. . . . He refuses to let anyone tell him he can't dream. That he won't make it. He believes in himself. He dedicates his life to his craft because he's finally realized that the work that you put in today has a direct and absolute impact on the life you live tomorrow."[8]

Cole's belief in himself paid off. Just like his first mixtape, his second was also well received by critics. A song from *The Warm Up* called "Lights Please" caught the attention of Jay-Z, and in 2009, Cole became the first artist signed to Roc Nation, Jay-Z's record label. Cole reflected on the experience, saying, "It's funny because one year after that [being rebuffed outside the studio] I was in his office because he had heard one of my songs and wanted to meet me. It was a really cool full-circle moment."[10]

While working away on his own music, Cole began making guest appearances on tracks by several musical artists, including Talib Kweli, Wale, and even Jay-Z himself. Cole appeared on the track "A Star Is Born" on *The Blueprint 3*, Jay-Z's chart-topping 2009 album. Cole was really on his way.

COLE'S WORLD CHANGES

Cole's star was rising. His fans were eager for his first full-length album on the Roc Nation label to come out. But Cole started feeling pressure because he had not been given a release date for his album. So he took matters into his own hands and headed to a recording studio in Times Square in New York. After all, he had what he considered to be a full album's worth of material ready to go. But Cole's new record label was not convinced that all the tracks Cole wanted to release would sell well, so he decided to put them on a mixtape instead. On November 12, 2010, he released a third mixtape, *Friday Night Lights*.

Cole self-produced almost all of *Friday Night Lights*. Reviewers had much to say about this mixtape. *Pitchfork* writer Tom Breihan described the tape as having "an organic warmth that lends it an immediate

Cole put out a lot of new music in 2010 and 2011.

ON THE ROAD

Part of being a successful musical artist these days involves touring and building one's fan base. During the spring and fall of 2010, Cole performed his music live on college campuses across the United States. On April 18, he sang "Dreams" from his mixtape *The Warm Up* and invited the audience at Vassar College in Poughkeepsie, New York, to join him during the hooks. At Cal State University's East Bay campus in Hayward, California, Cole gave an outdoor concert in October, and the audience also rapped along with him. Cole always makes a point of getting his audiences to sing along with him.

approachability."[1] However, some criticized parts of the album, saying they dragged, and some said certain rhymes did not work well. *SPIN* magazine's review praised the soulful beats of the tape, as well as Cole's freestyle raps over Timbaland and Kanye West hits. Writer Brandon Soderberg said the underdog theme was sometimes overdone on the album. Despite any criticisms, *Friday Night Lights* was a raging success. It was named Best Mixtape at the 2011 BET (Black Entertainment Television) Hip Hop Awards on October 11. Years later, some writers still consider this mixtape to be one of Cole's best releases to date.

COLE WORLD: THE SIDELINE STORY

After making three mixtapes, Cole experienced a transition as an artist while creating a proper full-length album. He said that the toughest part of making such an album was coming up with a statement that would tie the whole album together. Luckily, he had talented people to help him figure things out, including Mark Pitts and Jay-Z. They mentored Cole and helped him decide which material he should use, as he had more than he could possibly fit onto one album.

Cole's first single, "Who Dat"—and its accompanying music video—were released in the summer of 2010. This single peaked at Number 22 on the Billboard Mainstream R&B/Hip-Hop chart. The full album, titled *Cole World: The Sideline Story*, dropped on September 27, 2011. As with his mixtapes, Cole was heavily involved in the production of *Cole World*. He produced 13 of the album's 16 tracks.

Cole World: The Sideline Story became a big commercial success, opening at Number 1 on the Billboard 200 chart and selling more than 200,000 copies during its first week of release.[2] Many in the music industry were surprised at how well the album sold for a new artist, especially given Cole's "tepid radio presence."[3] *Pitchfork* writer

Jayson Greene celebrated the album's surprising musical details, such as the use of a grand piano, jazz guitars, and backup vocals.

Jay-Z appears on two tracks on the *Cole World* album. He can be heard in the intro of "Rise and Shine" as well as on the notably flashy track "Mr. Nice Watch."

MAD WORDSMITH SKILLS

One of Cole's talents is his ability to create meaningful songs that also have appealing rhythms. In the fast-paced, street-cool world of hip-hop, this is no small feat.

A great example of Cole's skills as a wordsmith can be found in his *Cole World* song "Sideline Story." In this song, Cole weaves two very different subjects, the game of basketball and a video game character from Mortal Kombat named Liu Kang, into the same metaphor: *"Throw flames, Liu Kang, the coach ain't help out, so I call my own shots."*[4]

"Sideline Story" also celebrates one of Cole's most popular themes, that of empowerment. His lyrics in the song state that people can't put limits on what he is going to be. One line says: "I'm breakin' out of my own box, you stay the same."[5] Perhaps he is referring to breaking out of the mold of what other rappers are like. Or he could be speaking about breaking out of the box of poverty in Fayetteville and making something great of himself.

STUDIO COLLABORATIONS

Besides working on his own album, Cole also made a number of guest appearances on other artists' albums. One of his biggest collaborations was the track "All I Want Is You," by American R&B artist Miguel. Released in May 2010, the song made it to Number 7 on *Billboard's* Hot R&B/ Hip-Hop Songs chart. Cole rapped at various points throughout the song and played a significant role in Miguel's music video for the track.

Cole also rapped on R&B artist Elle Varner's catchy song "Only Wanna Give It to You." Released on August 16, 2011, as a digital

WORKING WITH RIHANNA

Cole worked with superstar Rihanna on a couple of projects in 2011. Cole joined her Loud arena tour, which kicked off in June 2011. Performing on the tour gave Cole a chance to share his talent with audiences who might not have heard of him. Cole admitted to being nervous about opening for Rihanna, telling MTV News: "At first, I just thought I was in over my head. . . . But by the end of my show, I get the real cheers, like 'Oh, man! This guy's pretty good!'"[6]

On September 14, 2011, the music video for Cole's song "Can't Get Enough" debuted. The video was filmed in Barbados, which is Rihanna's native country. Here, Cole and Rihanna collaborated again, with Rihanna making a cameo appearance in the video.

download, the song was the debut single on Varner's album *Perfectly Imperfect*. Cole and Varner had met in college through a mutual friend. Two years later, Varner ran into Cole in the Sony building. In her words, "When it came time to do the lead single for my album, [Cole] was the first person I thought of."[7] The fun and colorful music video for "Only Wanna Give It to You" features Cole rapping and dancing alongside Varner.

The week of September 14, 2011, was a big one for Cole. That week he scored three hits on the *Billboard* R&B/Hip-Hop Songs chart—"Work Out," which was his own track; "Trouble," a collaboration with Bei Maejor; and "Only Wanna Give It to You."

HIGH PRAISE

Cole was in demand and proving himself a

THE DREAMVILLE FOUNDATION

In October 2011, Cole established the Dreamville Foundation as a way to lift the spirits of the urban youth of Fayetteville, North Carolina. The organization does a lot of great work, including donating thousands of dollars' worth of school supplies to kids who need assistance and taking children on field trips outside of their city neighborhoods. Cole's organization also hosts annual Dreamville Weekends, during which kids can take part in educational and fun-filled activities.

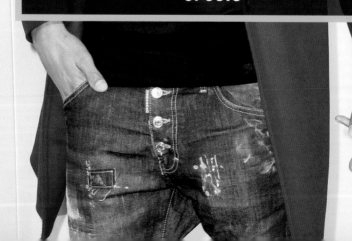

"Rhyme patterns are nothing without meanings to the words. . . . A lot of rappers can do those flows, but the raps aren't really about anything—which is cool sometimes, but to have the flow and the message is one of my favorite things."[8]

— J. Cole

> Cole's honors in 2012 included American Music Award nominations for New Artist of the Year and Favorite Rap/Hip-Hop Album.

rap superstar. In early October 2011, his debut album, *Cole World: The Sideline Story*, grabbed the Number 1 spot on the *Billboard 200*. After this news officially broke, Cole's Roc Nation boss Jay-Z praised the artist: "J. Cole's success is testament to amazing artist development and Cole's hard work. . . . I want to congratulate him on a #1 album and more importantly a great body of work."[9]

As if a Number 1 album was not enough, Cole was nominated twice at the 2012 BET Awards, in the categories Best Collaboration, for his work on the song "Party" with Beyoncé, and Best Male Hip-Hop Artist. Even though he did not win the awards, the nominations showed how highly others thought of his musical talents.

SINNER OR ORDINARY JOE?

With a Number 1 album under his belt, Cole was making a name for himself in the hip-hop world. One might wonder whether he felt pressure as he worked on his second album. After all, it is impossible to top Number 1. But Cole just kept his creative juices flowing, plugging away to create another great musical work. He released his new album, *Born Sinner*, on June 18, 2013.

Some people thought Cole was crazy to release his album the same day Kanye West's much-anticipated album *Yeezus* was slated to drop. Originally, *Born Sinner* had been scheduled for release on June 25. Cole was not looking to compete with West, but he wanted to make a point. Cole told MTV News, "This is art, and I can't compete against the Kanye West celebrity and the status that he's earned just from being a genius. . . . But I can put my name in the hat and tell you that I think my album

Cole performed with singer Jennifer Hudson at the Do Something Awards in 2013.

is great and you be the judge and you decide."[1] Cole's confidence was growing.

WORKING WITH CELEBRITIES

The same day that *Born Sinner* dropped, so did Cole's single "New York Times." Written by Cole, 50 Cent, and Bas, the song tells many tales of life in New York City—the good (getting an education), the bad (racism and segregation), and the ugly (shootings of African Americans in the city).

Cole was wowed to be working with such talented rappers. He also was impressed and pleasantly surprised at how respectful these rap giants were of his opinions. Cole told MTV News, "And [50 Cent is] like, 'No, this is your joint, you have to get it right. You've gotta tell me.' He was very adamant. I'll never forget that. Like it don't matter who you're in the

GOING OLD SCHOOL

Technology has become an essential part of the lyric-writing process for many rappers. They often type lyrics into their phones when writing new songs. But Cole went old school when writing *Born Sinner* and chose to use pen and paper rather than a phone or computer. He can trace his use of pen and paper to express his creativity back to his youth. As a teen, Cole wrote lyrics and stories in a notebook.

studio with—this is your product. I thought that was ill that he could sense I was tryna be respectful and was just like, 'nah we gon get it right.'"[2]

BORN SINNER—MORE TRACKS AND REVIEWS

Billboard writer Alex Gale called *Born Sinner* "stellar" and "easily the best hip-hop album of 2013."[3] He added that the album showed great improvement from Cole's previous one. Many, including Cole himself, have described *Born Sinner* as darker than his previous music. The 16 tracks deal with a range of topics, many of them very personal in nature, such as Cole struggling in the music industry, wrestling with his own demons, and dealing with depression.

> "This is an album about hip-hop ambition that's deeply skeptical about hip-hop ambition."[5]
> – Jon Caramanica, New York Times

Cole's track "Power Trip," featuring Miguel, was a huge hit that received lots of radio play. As *Billboard* writer Alex Gale noted, "It successfully introduced many of the sonic elements that tie 'Born Sinner' together: crunchy, jumpy Timbaland-inspired drums, deep rumbling bass, and soulful melodies."[4] Cole and Miguel both sing on the track, which reached Number 19 on the *Billboard* Hot 100 chart in July 2013. Another track from this album, "Crooked Smile," climbed the charts, making it as far as Number 27 in October 2013. This track featured rapper TLC, as well as a choir. Critics appreciated Cole's honest lyrics in this tune, as well as its "bouncy piano chords" and the vocal sample from DJ Khaled's "I'm on One."[6]

Cole performed at the 2013 BET Awards.

Cole toured widely in 2013 and 2014.

Born Sinner hit Number 1 on the *Billboard* 200 Chart in July 2013. The album also made it to the Top 10 in the United Kingdom during the summer of 2013. The London newspaper *Evening Standard* said, "He's found a niche as the voice of the ordinary Joe."[7]

EARNING NOTICE

Cole continued to tour. His Dollar & A Dream tour was
something special—and quite unusual. The ten-city tour
in support of *Born Sinner* started on June 11, 2013, in

Miami, Florida, a week before the album dropped. What made the tour unusual was that the dates and cities of the shows were announced in advance, but the venues were not. No tickets were sold ahead of time. Instead, entry was on a first-come, first-served basis. And in a world where concert tickets can cost hundreds of dollars, all tickets for this tour cost just one dollar.

Whether in concert venues or at award ceremonies, the world was clearly noticing Cole and his music. On June 30, 2013, he performed two songs at the BET Awards held at the Nokia Theater in Los Angeles, California. During his performance, Cole sat in the spotlight on a stool singing "Crooked Smile" as yellow lights enhanced the staging. His message

NOT MY STYLE

Fans today know Cole as a casual dresser, a rapper who is often seen in shorts and a T-shirt. But there was one time in particular when Cole went against his normal judgment, trying to fit the style profile of a big-time rapper. He reluctantly agreed to use a stylist for the 2013 BET Awards. The stylist dressed him in a loud black-and-gold Versace sweater, as well as a huge gold chain, gold watch, and gold bracelet. On the BET Awards red carpet, DJ Drama and Brandon T. Jackson wore the same sweater as Cole. Since that fashion mistake, Cole has done his own thing when it comes to style.

for the crowd, particularly the women, was one of self-love and acceptance rather than worrying about makeup and perfect hair and eyebrows.

Then Cole transitioned into "Power Trip." He moved about the stage as red and white lights flashed all around. His collaborator on the song, Miguel, also joined Cole as he performed the track to the very receptive audience.

REWARDING FANS AND GIVING BACK

In honor of his mixtape *The Warm Up's* fifth anniversary, Cole announced his second Dollar & A Dream tour on April 23, 2014. The shows began in July and continued through the summer. At one of the concerts on this tour, Cole performed his debut mixtape, *The Warm Up*, in its entirety. Cole's Dollar & A Dream tours gave access to the rap star to any fan who got in line early enough.

Besides working on his own albums and musical collaborations, Cole has also served as a mentor to up-and-coming musicians by establishing his own record label, Dreamville. The concept of Dreamville began back in 2007 when Cole and Ibrahim Hamad, his friend and former Saint John's classmate, came up with the idea.

However, Dreamville was officially formalized as a record label in 2014 with Hamad as president. The Dreamville website sums up the label's philosophy this way: "We are the label of the connected age. The creators of stories. Keeping a pulse on our community while exploring new sounds, new visuals and new ways to authentically and genuinely connect with all people, around the world."[9]

FERGUSON TO FOREST HILLS DRIVE

The summer of 2014 involved more for Cole than just making music and touring. In August, he traveled to Ferguson, Missouri, to pay his respects to Michael Brown, an African-American teenager who had been shot and killed by a white police officer on August 9. The shooting sparked protests that lasted for weeks.

While in Ferguson, Cole visited the place where Brown had been shot. Cole spoke with activists and protesters as a way to show his support. In addition, he visited the QuikTrip gas station where protests had turned into looting in the wake of Brown's death. Cole also brought a dozen of his Dreamville friends, paying for their tickets to travel to Ferguson. Cole said, "We came to talk, listen, and feel goosebumps and love amongst black people."[1]

Cole listens to the crowd during a 2014 concert in Chicago, Illinois.

The death of Michael Brown sparked protests across the country.

On August 15, just two days before his trip to Ferguson, Cole released the song "Be Free," which was a tribute to Michael Brown. Instead of rapping, Cole sings in a heartbreaking, haunting style over piano music. The song also includes audio from Dorian Johnson, a friend of

Brown's who was with him when he was shot. The lyrics of "Be Free" are powerful and reflect not only details of the events surrounding Michael Brown's death but also the struggles and violence many African Americans face today.

MAKING LIFE CHANGES

After releasing his two platinum albums, Cole started making some changes in his life. In June of 2014, he moved back to North Carolina and purchased his childhood home at 2014 Forest Hills Drive in Fayetteville. Cole had lived in the house as a tween and teenager. He tried to meditate as often as he could. Cole also wanted to create music that reflected his sense of creativity and his emotions, even when his ideas and feelings took his musical creations far away from his peers, the superstars of the hip-hop universe.

Cole released his third studio album, *2014 Forest Hills Drive*, on December 9, 2014. The album takes its name from Cole's childhood home. When asked to describe the album, Cole

"Can I attain major success but come out of this thing as myself?"[2]

– *J. Cole*

QUEST FOR PERFECTION

Cole is a perfectionist when it comes to the sound on his albums. To be sure he was happy with the sound quality on *2014 Forest Hills Drive*, Cole listened to it in a variety of ways before it was released. He checked out how it sounded through cheap headphones like the ones many people use. He also listened to the album on his laptop's speakers and through the sound system he had in his car.

said, "It's about a small town kid who has Hollywood dreams, goes there, realizes that something's wrong out there, so rather than being consumed by it and falling into the trap he goes back home."[3]

2014 Forest Hills Drive was unusual for a number of reasons. For starters, the album was announced just three weeks before it arrived in stores. It did not have the kind of normal promotional buildup that major labels generally use to ensure commercial success. And there had been no lead single, which record companies often use as a teaser to get fans excited about an artist's upcoming work. As *Atlantic* magazine writer Terrance Ross noted, "Cole has stopped trying to make radio-friendly singles—a complete reversal from last year's commercially successful *Born Sinner*."[4]

Cole's reputation and strong fan base made up for any lack of traditional promotion. In its first week out,

ON THE COVER

Cover art is a fun but important part of the product hip-hop artists share with their audiences. On his *2014 Forest Hills Drive* cover, Cole sits on top of his childhood home in Fayetteville. He wears simple, everyday-style clothes— pants, a sports jersey, and a pair of sneakers. Cole does not look at the photographer directly but instead looks lost in his thoughts as he gazes into the distance.

2014 Forest Hills Drive was streamed 15.7 million times on music service Spotify.[5]

Unlike Cole's previous albums, *2014 Forest Hills Drive* does not feature any guests, which is unusual in the hip-hop genre. Instead, *2014 Forest Hills Drive* seems to be more of a celebration of J. Cole and only J. Cole. As *Pitchfork* writer Craig Jenkins noted, "It's a block of Cole raps and Cole hooks served mostly over Cole beats."[6]

ALBUM TRACKS

2014 Forest Hills Drive has 13 tracks. As with most of Cole's releases, the topics on the album cover a lot of ground. He reflects on his place in the greater rap world on the growling track "Fire Squad." He raps: "Cole, you might be like the new Ice Cube meets the new Ice-T."[7] But Cole is not all swagger on this track, going on to question his own ability to win awards. "Fire Squad" reached Number 24 on the *Billboard* Hot Rap Songs chart.

"Apparently" is a song of contradictions. It relates Cole's mix of feelings during the time when he was enjoying his life as a college student at Saint John's, while at the same time his childhood home was foreclosed on, leaving his mother to find somewhere else to live.

This song proved to be the top single from *2014 Forest Hills Drive*. It climbed to Number 10 on the *Billboard* Rap Airplay chart. The piano arrangement on the track was compared to an Elton John song, a flattering comparison for any musician. The British music icon is known for his piano performances.

"No Role Modelz" also appeared on Billboard's Hot Rap Songs chart. The track criticizes gold-digging women and women who appear on reality television. Cole also talks about the lack of good role models for young people these days. The song uses a lot of insulting language toward women, leading one critic to say: "For all the talk of Cole's enlightenment he's a perfect brute when it comes to women, and 'No Role Modelz' is something of a tacit admission."[8]

ALBUM REVIEWS

"A deeply skilled empathizer, Cole can put *you* in *his* shoes too."[9]
– *Mikael Wood*, Los Angeles Times *music critic*

Reviews of *2014 Forest Hills Drive* were mixed, perhaps to an even greater degree than for his previous recordings. London's *Evening Standard* was pretty favorable to the album, saying that its new sound was richer and deeper than previous albums and featured "jazzy flourishes and the kind of sentiments you rarely hear in hip hop's bragging, grasping culture."[10]

The *Los Angeles Times* review said many good things about the album too. It mentioned Cole's honesty in his music, his ability to be self-critical, and how Cole comes alive when looking out at the larger world.

Other critics were less favorable. *Pitchfork*'s review was critical of Cole's decision not to have lead singles or guests on the album. It also questioned how the album tries to place Cole in the top tier of rap greats while also having him claim to be in touch with the common man. Whether good press or bad press, Cole's *2014 Forest Hills Drive* album was one that kept the music industry buzzing.

"ROAD TO HOMECOMING"

When Cole created *2014 Forest Hills Drive*, he also made a five-part mini-documentary series called the "Road to Homecoming." The segments aired weekly on HBO from mid-December 2015 until January 2016. The series shared some special moments from Cole's life during the previous year, including time spent on tour and hanging out with friends. The series was directed by Scott Lazar, and Cole served as one of the three executive producers. Executive producers have many jobs when working on films. For example, they make sure the film is finished on time, that it is made within the approved budget, and that the production meets the technical and artistic standards to which the studio has agreed. As Cole noted in a letter to his fans, this series gives viewers "some ill perspective on the inner-workings of my career and the important people that help make all this s*** happen."[1]

Cole performs in Atlanta, Georgia, in 2015.

LIFE ON THE ROAD

One might imagine that when a superstar such as Cole is on tour, he just performs, eats, and sleeps. But actually, Cole does a lot more than that. During his *2014 Forest Hills Drive* tour, he also worked on new beats. He was able to do this because his tour bus has a mini-studio with all kinds of recording equipment right there. He admitted that while he sometimes makes a few good beats in a row, on average only one out of every ten beats turns out great.

In addition to working on new beats, Cole took time out of his schedule for a little sightseeing while touring in Europe. He and several of his friends rode a gondola in the

> "I made the album that I'm so excited, and ecstatic about, like, to give to the world."[2]
>
> – *J. Cole*

A RARE INTERVIEW WITH COLE'S MOTHER

While Cole is known for keeping his personal life private, his mother, Kay, was interviewed for the HBO "Road to Homecoming" documentary. She said, "The things that inspired this album [*2014 Forest Hills Drive*] . . . to bring everything full circle . . . and turn something that was a bad memory into something so wonderful and positive, you know, that's his energy. You know what a positive person he is. I mean everything is just about positive energy."[3]

Riding in a gondola provides breathtaking views of the Swiss Alps.

Swiss Alps. With the snow-covered peaks, striking blue lakes, and goats grazing below, Cole compared the scene to something in a movie. Always one to have a sense of humor, he said to his friends, "I hate to sound like a cheesy old white lady, but that s*** is breathtaking, bro."[4] Never one to miss an opportunity for inspiration, Cole took out his notebook when the gondola stopped for a while and jotted down notes.

DISAPPOINTMENT . . . AND HAIR ADVICE

Cole's third Dollar & A Dream tour took place in late June 2015, in the midst of the Forest Hills Drive tour. Cole shared his thoughts about this four-city tour in the HBO mini-documentary, saying he felt disappointed that the venues were not bigger so more fans could attend the shows. He even tried to switch to a larger venue called Terminal 5 in New York, but it did not work out.

Rihanna came to one of the shows to see her friend Cole perform. After the show, she praised him at length, saying, "It was so good. I love seeing you like that. . . . This is the s*** they're gonna remember forever."[5] Then, in the joking manner of an old friend, she went on to give Cole advice about the best way to take care of his hair.

Rihanna is one of Cole's good friends.

HOMECOMING AND HIP-HOP ROYALTY

Cole ended his Forest Hills Drive tour on August 29 at the Crown Coliseum in his hometown of Fayetteville. The audience clearly loved the hometown hero, mouthing every lyric to every song he sang. Emotional fans broke into tears at various stages of the performance. Some cried because Cole's music connected with them personally. Others were moved to tears just seeing their beloved rapper performing live. As one concertgoer commented on film, "This is stuff we dreamed about. What people don't know is black performers don't get to perform in the Crown."[6]

Cole engaged the audience during every song of the show. Sometimes he did call-and-response with them. During his performance of "Power Trip," Cole let them sing multiple lines of the song while he danced and

HOT TOUR

Just weeks after his show at the Crown Coliseum, Cole hit another milestone in his career when he reached the Number 1 spot on *Billboard's* weekly tally of Hot Tours. During the third leg of his tour, from July 12 through September 4, Cole's tour earned $16.4 million. These concerts mainly took place in outdoor amphitheaters with just a small number of arena dates. Big Sean, Jeremih, and YG opened for Cole during this summertime leg of the Forest Hills Drive tour, performing for 473,961 fans in 29 cities.[7]

Cole mingles with some of his fans at a 2015 concert in New York City.

listened to thousands of his most loyal fans sing their hearts out. While Cole performed "Love Yourz," the Crown Coliseum was ablaze in the white lights of cell phones as everyone joined in the celebration of Cole's music and

message. Cole was also joined during this hometown concert by hip-hop greats Drake and Jay-Z. Both praised Cole and asked the audience to make some noise for him. The audience was more than happy to oblige.

RACKING UP MORE AWARDS

Cole's career was on fire. He was selling out arenas, making documentaries, and creating music that millions of people were buying. If that was not enough, he was also a nominee and a winner at some of the most prestigious award ceremonies for musical artists.

At the 2015 BET Awards, Cole was nominated for Best Male Hip-Hop Artist but lost to Kendrick Lamar. At the 2015 *Billboard* Music Awards, Cole had better luck. Although he lost Top Rap Artist to Iggy Azalea, he won Top Rap Album for *2014 Forest Hills Drive*. This was an especially impressive milestone in the hip-hop world since the album had no guest artists featured on its tracks.

In October 2015, Cole received many honors at the BET Hip Hop Awards. He was nominated for MVP of the Year, Lyricist of the Year, Producer of the

HIP-HOP GETS THE COLD SHOULDER

When many people think of music awards ceremonies, they picture their favorite artists coming up to the stage and giving acceptance speeches. But mainstream awards shows often do not devote much time during their broadcasts to hip-hop. Cole's 2015 *Billboard* Top Rap Album award was not televised, so his fans did not get a chance to see him give an acceptance speech.

Year, and Hustler of the Year. Two of his songs were also nominated for Impact Track: "Apparently" and "Be Free." In the end, Cole came away from this ceremony the winner of Best Live Performer and Album of the Year for *2014 Forest Hills Drive*.

The following year proved to be huge for Cole as well. He won Impact Track for his song "Love Yourz" at the 2016 BET Hip Hop Awards. He was also nominated for Lyricist of the Year and Best Live Performer at the same event. And, although he did not win, Cole was nominated for three Grammys—Best Rap Album for *2014 Forest Hills Drive*, Best Rap Performance for "Apparently," and Best R&B Performance for "Planes," a song by Jeremih featuring Cole.

J. COLE VERSUS DRAKE

During the course of his career, Cole has competed against Drake in a number of awards categories. For example, at the 2015 BET Hip Hop Awards, Cole lost to Drake in the category MVP of the Year but won against Drake in the Best Live Performer category. And at the 2015 BET Awards, both Cole and Drake were competitors but lost to Kendrick Lamar. In 2016, Cole competed against Drake again at the BET Awards for Best Male Hip Hop Artist, but Drake won. And at the 2017 *Billboard* Music Awards, Cole was nominated for Top Rap Artist and for Top Rap Album for *4 Your Eyez Only* but lost both times to Drake. Regardless of their competition at award ceremonies, the two artists speak highly of each other and guest perform at each other's shows.

4 YOUR EYEZ ONLY

Winning awards is exciting for any musical artist. But Cole was not content to just rely on such honors. He put his heart and soul into his fourth studio album, titled *4 Your Eyez Only*, which was released on December 9, 2016—exactly two years after the release of *2014 Forest Hills Drive*.

As with his previous album, Cole did not have a lead single or big promotional campaign prior to the release of *4 Your Eyez Only*. Some fans discovered the album was coming out by finding the preorder page on iTunes. Others may have been closely watching the Dreamville website in search of news of the latest Cole release.

But no matter how Cole's fans found out about *4 Your Eyez Only*, they could not wait to get their hands on it. In its first week of sales, it had the third-largest opening

Cole connects with the crowd during his concerts.

Cole commands the stage during a 2016 concert in Queens, New York.

week for any album in 2016. By April 2017, the album was certified platinum.

WHAT'S THE ALBUM ABOUT?

4 Your Eyez Only is not a dance-party type of hip-hop album. Instead, it grapples with many weighty themes,

including life, death, and how people are connected. As a Billboard article stated, *"4 Your Eyez Only* is a personal conversation, first and foremost, with Cole himself."[1] Apple Music Preview also described the album: "At center stage with no featured guests, the North Carolina rapper speaks out on social ills, black lives, and doing the right thing in a world of wrong."[2]

Cole chose to narrate the album through a character who is a mash-up of two men he grew up with in Fayetteville. Despite his tough, in-trouble-with-the-law persona, the character is also full of love for his family and friends. Cole said the goal of the album was "to humanize the people that have been villainized in the media."[3]

Music critics found much to discuss in terms of the thematic material of *4 Your Eyez Only*. One *Pitchfork* critic was impressed with the lyrical content, saying that the album featured "some of Cole's most affecting writing to date."[4]

In terms of its sound, *Billboard* writer Sowmya Krishnamurthy described the work as a "stripped-down, lyrically-focused album."[5] Strings and jazz touches give the various tracks a more settled feeling than some of Cole's other recordings. The album also relies on Cole's singing voice—as opposed to his rapping voice—more than his previous albums. Some critics found the production on this album to be of a lesser quality than that of *2014 Forest Hills Drive* and describe some of the tracks in the middle of the album as "sleepy."[6]

SELECTED TRACKS

The ten tracks on *4 Your Eyez Only* are a fascinating mix for Cole fans. All ten songs made it to at least Number 34 on the *Billboard* Hot 100 chart, with "Deja Vu" reaching the Number 7 spot.

"Neighbors" is a powerful song that tells the story of how Sheltuh, the studio where Cole recorded this album, was raided by police in March 2016. Cole has wondered if this happened because a neighbor thought the building was a drug den.

Many have wondered if the track "4 Your Eyez Only" is about the passing of Cole's friend James McMillan Jr. Some verses of this song seem to be a conversation between Cole and his friend's daughter: "One day your daddy called me, told me he had a funny feeling / What he'd been dealing with lately he wasn't telling."[7]

Not all the tracks on *4 Your Eyez Only* are dark, however. Some are hopeful, perhaps even joyful. Cole celebrates the happiness brought by home life in the song "Foldin Clothes": "I know you tired so I wonder how I can help . . . Oh I wanna fold clothes for you."[8]

ANOTHER DOCUMENTARY

Following the success of the "Road to Homecoming" documentary series, Cole made another documentary for HBO, "J. Cole: 4 Your Eyez Only." The 48-minute film premiered on April 15, 2017. It features performances from the *4 Your Eyez Only* album and interviews with residents from various places, including Atlanta, Georgia; Baton Rouge, Louisiana; and Ferguson, Missouri.

Cole spoke with many people while making this film but always with the humble manner of a regular guy, not a superstar rapper. After talking at length with a woman in Jonesboro, Arkansas, Cole hugged her and expressed his condolences on the loss of her child from gun violence. The film also shares the story of a worker at a low-budget hotel who said how important it was to have compassion for others.

J. Cole described the documentary's goal this way: "I felt like it would be mad powerful for black people to see black people talking to each other. . . . See how human they are, and see black men walk around with their daughters, and get a whole different perspective. . . . If I'm listening, why can't you listen?"[9]

MARRIAGE AND FAMILY

Cole is not one to share the details of his private life on social media or to tweet about his personal business. In 2015, he secretly married his longtime girlfriend

WHO IS MELISSA HEHOLT?

Melissa Heholt has been an important part of Cole's life for well over a decade. She and Cole met during their time at Saint John's University and have been together ever since. She earned a master's degree in childhood education and taught for a while but changed her career path and became an event planner. She runs her own company, called Statice Events, and plans everything from weddings and birthday parties to product launches. Like her husband, Heholt is very private.

Melissa Heholt. The two met when they were students at Saint John's University in New York. Rumors had circulated about the couple being engaged, but it was not until Cole was caught off-guard by an interviewer in January 2016 that his marriage was confirmed.

"I feel like relationships are a beautiful thing, period."[11]
– J. Cole

Cole was not only secretly married but had also become a father. He did not share much about this big news, but many sources have indicated that Cole's baby is a girl. He sang about his bundle of joy on the strings-and-baby-crying-filled track "She's Mine—Part 2": "You are now the reason that I fight / I ain't never did nothing this right in my whole life."[10]

chapter NINE

THE MAN AND THE MESSAGE

From his humble origins, Cole has rocketed himself into the hip-hop stratosphere, working tirelessly to create music that will likely inspire others for generations to come. He stands as a testament to the power of hard work and not giving up on one's dreams. He has shown his fans that it is cool to work hard at school and to value education, even when many other rappers just celebrate money and status.

A "HIP-HOP WORDSMITH"

One way that Cole has had an impact on hip-hop and the larger music scene is through his work as a lyricist. Writer Leonard Moore referred to Cole as a "hip-hop wordsmith" in 2017.[1] From his use of metaphors to his incredible rhyme sequences, Cole has crafted lines in his songs that have both maximum impact and excellent rhythm. As an

Cole reached new heights of artistic success in 2016 and 2017.

article in London's *Evening Standard* noted, "He's a calm, clear, unshowy rapper, great on internal rhyme schemes and honesty. You don't come to his songs to escape, you come for the truth."[2]

This lyrical honesty is also a part of the huge influence of Cole's music on hip-hop. While some rappers rely heavily on name-dropping and bragging about their jet-setting lifestyles, Cole takes some risks in tunes such as "Foldin Clothes." In this song, he pokes fun at himself for drinking almond milk but also shows that his life is real and relatable.

STAYING TRUE TO HIMSELF

Cole has created a unique but very successful niche for himself in the hip-hop world by presenting himself as an everyday kind of guy. Through his music videos, documentaries, and print interviews, and even onstage at arena tours, Cole reminds his fans of his humble origins. He has

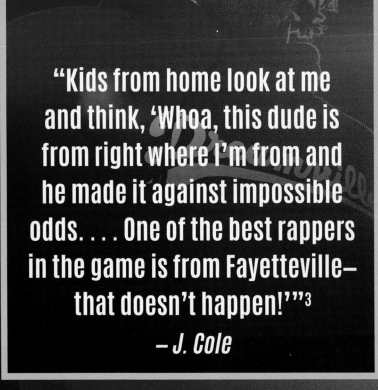

"Kids from home look at me and think, 'Whoa, this dude is from right where I'm from and he made it against impossible odds. . . . One of the best rappers in the game is from Fayetteville—that doesn't happen!'"[3]

— *J. Cole*

been described as a rapper who is not worried about impressing people. As Cole noted, "It's about growing up and realizing. . . . 'Yo. I really do like myself being a regular person who could be [somebody's] homeboy.'"[4]

After he saw kids at his concerts sporting fancy jewelry and expensive watches, Cole made a choice. He wanted to be a kind of hip-hop artist to whom more kids could really relate. In most of his concert footage, he wears a T-shirt, sneakers, and shorts or sweats. Rather than feeling offended if someone says he is a regular guy, he sees it as a great compliment.

This humility also shows itself when Cole deals with members of the press. While it is common for rappers to show up for interviews hours behind schedule—in what is known as "hip-hop time"—Cole recently asked an interviewer to come ahead of schedule because Cole was running early. Cole

A DIVERSE FAN BASE

Among Cole's many talents is his ability to connect with a wide variety of listeners. Professional basketball star Kevin Durant commented not only on Cole's ability to rap but also on his ability to play basketball. Hip-hop mogul Jay-Z has hinted that Cole has a long future in the music industry, saying, "He's gonna be here as long as he wants to do it, as long as he's inspired." Even former president Barack Obama sang Cole's praises when he said simply, "I love J. Cole."[5]

showed up without an entourage, wearing jogging pants, a sweater, and no jewelry. In a world of big-ego celebrities, Cole has proven to be a breath of fresh air.

SUPPORTING HIS FANS

Cole is known as one of the most generous members of the hip-hop community. He has given to his fans and community members in many ways. His Dollar & A Dream tours have allowed fans from all over the United States to see their hero perform for just one dollar. In an era when musicians make millions of dollars on concert ticket sales, this is a unique offer for fans.

EXPRESSING GRATITUDE

Whether live onstage or in letters published online and in magazines, Cole has shown he is grateful for how far he has come. At his sold-out Madison Square Garden concert, he asked the audience to let him just soak in the moment before continuing his performance. In a 2014 letter printed in *Vibe* magazine, Cole celebrated his journey as an artist: "In 5 years I have come so far. I am grateful to be here today, alive and full of potential. But I am not satisfied. I still want more. I still have dreams, even bigger now than before."[6]

Cole has also supported his fans though some grassroots album promotion. Before *2014 Forest Hills Drive* was released, Cole held a contest whereby a handful of winners got to travel to the home in which Cole grew up in Fayetteville and preview the album. Cole's longtime friend and manager Ibrahim Hamad said Cole has a special relationship with his followers: "Fans stuck around since day one. They love him and believe in him. We realized if we take care of our fans and give them what they want, they'll spread the gospel of J. Cole."[7] Fans repaid Cole's many kindnesses by buying hundreds of thousands of copies in the album's first week.

Cole has often gone the extra mile to do special things for his fans. When one of his followers on Twitter asked Cole to sign her CD, he traveled from New York to Philadelphia, Pennsylvania, to sign her copy of *2014 Forest Hills Drive*. (Cole had told fans to tweet him pictures of themselves holding his CD and that he would come to sign them.) He also has connected with students on college campuses all over the United States, including a surprise visit to Morehouse

A DREAM COME TRUE

In 2015, Cole was in Dallas, Texas. One of his Twitter followers told him she wanted to see him. He replied, "Send me DM [direct message] with your address. I'll come play u the album."[8] Not long afterward, Cole and his crew showed up at the fan's house in Dallas, played video games with her younger family members, and hung out with them. And the fan got to check out his new album—*2014 Forest Hills Drive*—even before it hit store shelves.

College in Atlanta, Georgia, in November 2015. During the Morehouse College visit, Cole answered questions about all kinds of topics, including his role as a speaker on race relations.

BUILDING CAREERS

Cole has helped to build the careers of several up-and-coming musicians through his record label Dreamville. He has also acted as a mentor, providing advice to these fellow artists. Ari Lennox, the first woman signed to the Dreamville label, had wonderful things to say about Cole and his team: "Cole is really awesome. . . . For my EP, Cole was the one who fought for 'La, La, La' . . . it was really cool that Cole actually cared about that aspect [Lennox's singing on that track] and making sure that was highlighted."[9]

SOCIAL MEDIA

Throughout his career, Cole has been very selective about his use of social media. When he does use social media, it is not typically to brag or to sell anything. In December 2015, he tweeted that he was at Louisiana State University in Baton Rouge playing football and basketball and told fans to "pull up."[10] Students quickly found him and joined the superstar for a game of pickup football. After the game, he chatted with fans and signed some autographs. As a 2014 *Vibe* article stated, "J. Cole's brand is very reserved. Because he doesn't tweet or Instagram much, it's more special when he says something. People have to pay attention."[11]

Cole, *center*, performs with Bas, *right*, while promoting his Dreamville Foundation.

In addition to Lennox, Cole has signed other artists to his Dreamville label who have turned into hot, award-winning hip-hop acts. Bas, Omen, and Cozz have all released albums under the Dreamville imprint. Cole and Hamad have been striving to build careers, not just put out flashy music for the present.

GIVING BACK

Charity work has been an important part of Cole's life
as he has climbed the ladder to success. His Dreamville
Foundation aims to set young people up for success
through book clubs and other events. It also lets kids meet

people who have jobs they might never have considered trying themselves. As Cole said, "I want to start the process of showing them there are other options besides what's on the screen. They don't have to be a rapper or an athlete; there are people who manage the rappers, who book the shows. There are so many jobs you can do; this is about expanding their minds to those possibilities."[12]

In addition to his foundation's work, Cole has also given back to the Fayetteville community in other ways. In June 2014, he bought the house he grew up in on Forest Hills Drive, not to live there himself but to provide single mothers and their children with rent-free housing. Cole's idea was that every two years, a new family would move into his childhood home so they could improve their financial situation. Outside of Fayetteville, Cole also has continued to talk to students at various colleges

Rather than shy away from social justice issues, Cole uses his lyrics and his clothing to draw attention to racial profiling and police brutality in the United States.

around the country. An example is his November 2014 visit to New York's Columbia University, where he ran a question-and-answer session about the music business.

WHAT IS NEXT?

Cole is a man with ambition and a strong work ethic. During his "Homecoming" documentary, he said he wished he had more time or more passion to do something such as run for mayor or the city council in Fayetteville. He added, "I don't think I do enough, honestly."[13]

It is hard to guess what is next for Cole, as he often keeps his projects under wraps. Many outlets have mentioned that Cole and Kendrick Lamar were working on a collaborative project, though details remained scarce in the summer of 2017. It is likely that Cole will continue to work on his own tracks while also collaborating with a diverse group of musicians. He will also continue to tour. His 57-date, *4 Your Eyez Only* world tour kicked off in June 2017 and went until December, making stops from Norway to Australia. With a fan base that stretches around the globe, Cole's music will continue to inspire listeners for years to come.

1985

On January 28, Jermaine Lamarr Cole is born in Frankfurt, West Germany.

1996

Jermaine and his family move to a house on Forest Hills Drive in Fayetteville, North Carolina.

1997

Jermaine starts rapping, first using the name Blaza and then Therapist.

2003

Jermaine graduates from Terry Sanford High School in Fayetteville.

2007

After attending Saint John's University for four years, Cole graduates with honors in May; on May 4, Cole releases his first mixtape, *The Come Up*; he later signs with his first record label, Sony/Jive.

2009

On June 15, Cole releases his second mixtape, *The Warm Up*; he is the first artist signed to the Roc Nation record label.

2010

On November 12, Cole's third mixtape, *Friday Night Lights*, is released.

2011

On September 27, Cole's debut album, *Cole World: The Sideline Story*, is released; on October 11, Cole's album *Friday Night Lights* is named Best Mixtape at the Black Entertainment Television (BET) Hip Hop Awards.

2012

Cole is nominated for Best Collaboration and Best Male Hip-Hop Artist at the BET Awards.

2013

On June 11, Cole begins his first Dollar & A Dream tour, in which tickets cost just one dollar; on June 18, Cole releases the *Born Sinner* album.

2014

In June, Cole purchases his childhood home at 2014 Forest Hills Drive in Fayetteville; in July, Cole begins his second Dollar & A Dream tour; on December 9, his third album, *2014 Forest Hills Drive*, is released.

2015

On August 4, Cole plays to a sold-out crowd at Madison Square Garden; he marries his college sweetheart, Melissa Heholt; his daughter is born.

2016

On December 9, Cole's album *4 Your Eyez Only* is released.

2017

Cole kicks off his *4 Your Eyes Only* world tour in June.

FULL NAME

Jermaine Lamarr Cole

DATE OF BIRTH

January 28, 1985

PLACE OF BIRTH

Frankfurt, West Germany

PARENT

Kay Cole

EDUCATION

- 2003 graduate of Terry Sanford High School

- 2007 graduate of Saint John's University

MARRIAGE

Melissa Heholt

CHILDREN

Name unknown

CAREER HIGHLIGHTS

J. Cole has had four albums go platinum. As of 2016, he has won five BET Hip Hop Awards, as well as numerous other honors, including the 2015 Billboard Music Award for Top Rap Album.

ALBUMS

The Come Up (2007), *The Warm Up* (2009), *Friday Night Lights* (2010), *Cole World: The Sideline Story* (2011), *2014 Forest Hills Drive* (2014), *4 Your Eyez Only* (2016)

CONTRIBUTION TO HIP-HOP

Among Cole's many contributions to hip-hop is his expansion of the topics covered in hip-hop lyrics. For example, his music has tackled subjects such as mental health, racism, and the media's impact on women's self-image. Cole has also collaborated with a wide range of artists, including Jay-Z, Kendrick Lamar, Drake, and Elle Varner.

CONFLICTS

As a child, Cole grew up poor. He sometimes lived in neighborhoods where he did not feel safe. His family did not always have enough money for food. Cole had conflict with his stepfather, who was not a kind, supportive figure in his life.

QUOTE

"Can I attain major success but come out of this thing as myself?"

—*J. Cole*

CALL-AND-RESPONSE

When one artist delivers a song line and a second answers back.

DEBUT

The first album or publication by a musician or group.

GENRE

A category of artistic composition, such as in music, characterized by similar styles, forms, or subject matter.

HOOK

A catchy part of a song (but not necessarily the chorus) that draws in a listener.

ICONIC

Having the characteristics of someone or something that is very famous or popular.

MAGNA CUM LAUDE

A term meaning "with great distinction" used in reference to college degrees or diplomas.

METAPHOR

A figure of speech that compares two objects or ideas.

MIXING

Combining a number of recorded soundtracks or separate signals when making an album.

MIXTAPE

A compilation of unreleased tracks, freestyle rap music, and DJ mixes of songs.

PLATINUM

An album is certified platinum when it sells a million units.

PRODUCER

The person who supervises the sampling, mixing, and recording of music and also guides the performer.

R&B

Rhythm and blues; a type of pop music of African-American origin that has a soulful vocal style and that features improvisation.

RAP

A type of music in which words are recited quickly and rhythmically, often over an electronic, prerecorded backing.

SAMPLE

A piece of recorded music used by DJs or producers to make new music.

SELECTED BIBLIOGRAPHY

"J. Cole: An Upstart Rapper Speaks for Himself." *NPR*. NPR. 1 November 2011. Web. 11 Sept. 2017.

Krishnamurthy, Sowmya. "From St. John's University to Madison Square Garden, J. Cole Comes Home." *Village Voice*. Village Voice. Web. 11 Sept. 2017.

Smyth, David. "The Gentle Rapper: J Cole Interview." *Evening Standard*. Evening Standard. 9 Dec. 2014. Web. 11 Sept. 2017.

FURTHER READINGS

Burling, Alexis. *Drake: Hip-Hop Superstar*. Minneapolis: Abdo, 2018. Print.

Cummings, Judy Dodge. *The Men of Hip-Hop*. Minneapolis: Abdo, 2017. Print.

Klepeis, Alicia Z. *Kanye West: Music Industry Influencer*. Minneapolis: Abdo, 2018. Print.

ONLINE RESOURCES

Booklinks
NONFICTION NETWORK
FREE! ONLINE NONFICTION RESOURCES

To learn more about J. Cole, visit **abdobooklinks.com**. These links are routinely monitored and updated to provide the most current information available.

MORE INFORMATION

For more information on this subject, contact or visit the following organizations:

DREAMVILLE FOUNDATION

thedreamvillefoundation.org

The Dreamville Foundation is J. Cole's nonprofit organization geared to help the urban youth of Fayetteville, North Carolina.

ROCK & ROLL HALL OF FAME

1100 Rock and Roll Boulevard
Cleveland, Ohio, 44114
216-781- 7625
rockhall.com/learn

The Rock & Roll Hall of Fame is a museum located in Cleveland, Ohio. It has exhibits that feature a number of rappers and hip-hop artists.

SOURCE NOTES

CHAPTER 1. A SOLD-OUT SHOW

1. Alyssa Bishop. "Nobody's Perfect – J. Cole *Forest Hills Drive* August 4, 2015 MSG." *YouTube*. YouTube, 4 Aug. 2015. Web. 11 Sept. 2017.

2. LMG Touring. "J. Cole's *Forest Hills Drive* Tour." *LiveDesign*. Penton, 25 Mar. 2016. Web. 11 Sept. 2017.

3. Adelle Platon. "Review: 10 Thoughts on J. Cole's *2014 Forest Hills Drive* Tour." *Vibe*. Billboard-Hollywood Reporter, 6 Aug. 2015. Web. 11 Sept. 2017.

4. "LMG Touring. "J. Cole's *Forest Hills Drive* Tour." *LiveDesign*. Penton, 25 March 2016. Web. 11 Sept. 2017.

5. 50 Cent. "I Get Money." *Genius*. Genius Media Group, n.d. Web. 11 Sept. 2017.

6. Alyssa Bishop. "What St. Tropez Is About – J. Cole *Forest Hills Drive* August 4, 2015 MSG." *YouTube*. YouTube, 4 Aug. 2015. Web. 11 Sept. 2017.

7. Ibid.

8. J. Cole. "Love Yourz." *Genius*. Genius Media Group, n.d. Web. 11 Sept. 2017.

9. J. Cole. "Crooked Smile." *Google Play Music*. Universal Music Publishing Group, n.d. Web. 11 Sept. 2017.

10. Nellii Jean. "J. Cole – Love Yourz (live@MSG)." *YouTube*. YouTube, 13 Aug. 2015. Web. 11 Sept. 2017.

11. Sowmya Krishnamurthy. "From St. John's University to Madison Square Garden, J. Cole Comes Home." *Village Voice*. Village Voice, 28 July 2015. Web. 11 Sept. 2017.

12. Ibid.

13. Bob Allen. "J. Cole Leads Hot Tours Tally, Taylor Swift's Trek Surpasses $150M Mark." *Billboard*. Billboard-Hollywood Reporter Media Group, 24 Sept. 2015. Web. 11 Sept. 2017.

CHAPTER 2. FINDING HIS MUSIC

1. "J. Cole: An Upstart Rapper Speaks for Himself." *NPR*. NPR, 1 Nov. 2011. Web. 11 Sept. 2017.

2. Ibid.

3. David Smyth. "The Gentle Rapper: J. Cole Interview." *Evening Standard*. Evening Standard, 9 Dec. 2014. Web. 11 Sept. 2017.

4. "J. Cole Talks Rough Childhood on *2014 Forest Hills Drive*." *Music Times*. Music Times, 9 Dec. 2014. Web. 11 Sept. 2017.

5. Caitlin Carter. "J. Cole Gives Tour of Childhood Home, 2014 Forest Hills Drive, Fayetteville, North Carolina, in New Video." *Music Times*. Music Times, 24 Nov. 2014. Web. 11 Sept. 2017.

6. Power 106 FM. "J. Cole Speaks on His First Job Ever." *YouTube*. YouTube, 13 June 2013. Web. 11 Sept. 2017.

7. Insanul Ahmed. "25 Things You Didn't Know about J. Cole." *Complex*. Complex Media, 10 June 2013. Web. 11 Sept. 2017.

8. "J. Cole: An Upstart Rapper Speaks for Himself." *NPR*. NPR, 1 Nov. 2011. Web. 11 Sept. 2017.

9. "J. Cole Gives Us a Tour of 2014 Forest Hills Drive in Fayetteville, N.C." *YouTube*. YouTube, 24 Nov. 2014. Web. 2 Oct. 2017.

10. Insanul Ahmed. "25 Things You Didn't Know about J. Cole." *Complex*. Complex Media, 10 June 2013. Web. 11 Sept. 2017.

CHAPTER 3. COLLEGE DAYS AND MIXTAPES

1. Natalie Weiner. "The Oral History of J. Cole's Basketball Career." *Bleacher Report*. Bleacher Report, 19 Apr. 2017. Web. 11 Sept. 2017.

2. Insanul Ahmed. "25 Things You Didn't Know about J. Cole." *Complex*. Complex Media, 10 June 2013. Web. 11 Sept. 2017.

3. Andy Morris. "GQ&A: J. Cole." *GQ*. Condé Nast, 29 Mar. 2012. Web. 11 Sept. 2017.

4. Sowmya Krishnamurthy. "From St. John's University to Madison Square Garden, J. Cole Comes Home." *Village Voice*. Village Voice, 28 July 2015. Web. 11 Sept. 2017.

5. Ibid.

6. "J. Cole Speaks on His Production Abilities, *The Warm Up*." *HipHopDX*. HipHopDX, 4 May 2010. Web. 11 Sept. 2017.

7. Rob Markman. "Jay-Z Congratulates J. Cole on #1 Album." *MTV News*. Viacom International, 5 Oct. 2011. Web. 11 Sept. 2017.

8. Iyana Robertson. "J. Cole Commemorates *The Warm Up*'s 5-Year Anniversary with an Open Letter." *Vibe*. Billboard-Hollywood Reporter Media Group, 15 June 2014. Web. 11 Sept. 2017.

9. Sowmya Krishnamurthy. "From St. John's University to Madison Square Garden, J. Cole Comes Home." *Village Voice*. Village Voice, 28 July 2015. Web. 11 Sept. 2017.

10. David Smyth. "The Gentle Rapper: J. Cole Interview." *Evening Standard*. Evening Standard, 9 Dec. 2014. Web. 11 Sept. 2017.

CHAPTER 4. COLE'S WORLD CHANGES

1. Tom Breihan. "J. Cole: *Friday Night Lights*." *Pitchfork*. Condé Nast, 29 Nov. 2010. Web. 11 Sept. 2017.

2. "J. Cole's *Cole World: The Sideline Story* First Week Sales Are In." *Uproxx*. Uproxx, 5 Oct. 2011. Web. 11 Sept. 2017.

3. Jayson Greene. "*Cole World: The Sideline Story*." *Pitchfork*. Condé Nast, 30 Sept. 2011. Web. 11 Sept. 2017.

4. J. Cole. "*Sideline Story*." *Genius*. Genius Media Group, n.d. Web. 11 Sept. 2017.

5. Ibid.

6. "Rihanna and Opening Act J. Cole Are a 'Great Fit.'" *MTV News*. Viacom International, 26 July 2011. Web. 11 Sept. 2017.

7. Brooklyne Gipson. "Elle Varner Debuts New Video on 106 and Park." *BET*. BET Interactive, 4 Oct. 2011. Web. 11 Sept. 2017.

8. "J. Cole: An Upstart Rapper Speaks for Himself." *NPR*. NPR, 1 Nov. 2011. Web. 11 Sept. 2017.

9. Rob Markman. "Jay-Z Congratulates J. Cole on #1 Album." *MTV News*. Viacom International, 5 Oct. 2011. Web. 11 Sept. 2017.

CHAPTER 5. SINNER OR ORDINARY JOE?

1. Nadeska Alexis. "J. Cole Went Head-To-Head with Kanye because 'My Album Is Great.'" *MTV News*. Viacom International, 20 June 2013. Web. 11 Sept. 2017.

2. Nadeska Alexis. "50 Cent Challenged J. Cole 'to Get It Right' in the *Born Sinner* Studio." *MTV News*. Viacom International, 19 June 2013. Web. 11 Sept. 2017.

3. Alex Gale. "J. Cole, 'Born Sinner': Track-By-Track Review." *Billboard*. Billboard-Hollywood Reporter Media Group, 7 June 2013. Web. 11 Sept. 2017.

4. Ibid.

5. Jon Caramanica. "Online Upstarts Nod to Convention." *New York Times*. New York Times Company, 26 June 2013. Web. 12 Sept. 2017.

6. Alex Gale. "J. Cole, *Born Sinner*: Track-By-Track Review." *Billboard*. Billboard-Hollywood Reporter Media Group, 7 June 2013. Web. 11 Sept. 2017.

CONTINUED

7. David Smyth. "The Gentle Rapper: J. Cole Interview." *Evening Standard*. Evening Standard, 9 Dec. 2014. Web. 12 Sept. 2017.

8. Iyana Robertson. "J. Cole Commemorates *The Warm Up*'s 5-Year Anniversary with an Open Letter." *Vibe*. Billboard-Hollywood Reporter, 15 June 2014. Web. 11 Sept. 2017.

9. "Welcome to Dreamville." *Dreamville*. Dreamville Foundation, n.d. Web. 12 Sept. 2017.

CHAPTER 6. FERGUSON TO FOREST HILLS DRIVE

1. "J. Cole Talks about His Visit to Ferguson and Shares His Thoughts on Michael Brown." *YouTube*. YouTube, 19 Aug. 2014. Web. 12 Sept. 2017.

2. Sowmya Krishnamurthy. "From St. John's University to Madison Square Garden, J. Cole Comes Home." *Village Voice*. Village Voice, 28 July 2015. Web. 11 Sept. 2017.

3. David Smyth. "The Gentle Rapper: J. Cole Interview." *Evening Standard*. Evening Standard, 9 Dec. 2014. Web. 12 Sept. 2017.

4. Terrance F. Ross. "J. Cole: Still a Classic Album Away from Greatness." *Atlantic*. Atlantic Monthly Group, 14 Dec. 2014. Web. 12 Sept. 2017.

5. Joe Coscarelli. "J. Cole Hits No. 1." *New York Times*. New York Times Company, 17 Dec. 2014. Web. 12 Sept. 2017.

6. Craig Jenkins. "J. Cole: *2014 Forest Hills Drive*." *Pitchfork*. Condé Nast, 11 Dec. 2014. Web. 12 Sept. 2017.

7. Mikael Wood. "Review: J. Cole's *2014 Forest Hills Drive* Hits Authentic Notes." *Los Angeles Times*. Los Angeles Times, 8 Dec. 2014. Web. 12 Sept. 2017.

8. Craig Jenkins. "J. Cole: *2014 Forest Hills Drive*." *Pitchfork*. Condé Nast, 11 Dec. 2014. Web. 12 Sept. 2017.

9. Mikael Wood. "Review: J. Cole's *2014 Forest Hills Drive* Hits Authentic Notes." *Los Angeles Times*. Los Angeles Times, 8 Dec. 2014. Web. 12 Sept. 2017.

10. David Smyth. "The Gentle Rapper: J. Cole Interview." *Evening Standard*. Evening Standard, 9 Dec. 2014. Web. 12 Sept. 2017.

CHAPTER 7. "ROAD TO HOMECOMING"

1. Camille Augustin. "J. Cole Releases Part 2 of Mini-Documentary, 'Road to Homecoming: Ain't Nothing Like That.'" *Vibe*. Billboard-Hollywood Reporter Media Group, 23 Dec. 2015. Web. 2 Oct. 2017.

2. "Road to Homecoming: Episode 1." *HBO*. HBO, Web. n.d. 12 Sept. 2017.

3. Ibid.

4. "Road to Homecoming: Episode 2." *HBO*. HBO, Web. n.d. 12 Sept. 2017.

5. "Road to Homecoming: Episode 3." *HBO*. HBO, Web. n.d. 12 Sept. 2017.

6. Kris Ex. "J. Cole Is a Fitting Hometown Hero in 'Forest Hills Drive: Homecoming' HBO Special: Review." *Billboard*. Billboard-Hollywood Reporter Media Group, 11 Jan. 2016. Web. 12 Sept. 2017.

7. Bob Allen. "J. Cole Leads Hot Tours Tally, Taylor Swift's Trek Surpasses $150M Mark." *Billboard*. Billboard-Hollywood Reporter Media Group, 24 Sept. 2015. Web. 11 Sept. 2017.

CHAPTER 8. 4 YOUR EYEZ ONLY

1. Sowmya Krishnamurthy. "J. Cole Contemplates Life & Death on *4 Your Eyez Only*." *Billboard*. Billboard-Hollywood Reporter Media Group, 14 Dec. 2016. Web. 12 Sept. 2017.

2 "Apple Music Preview: *4 Your Eyez Only*." *Apple*. Apple, 2017. Web. 24 Sept. 2017.

3. Jon Caramanica. "J. Cole, the Platinum Rap Dissident, Steps Back from the Spotlight." *New York Times*. New York Times Company, 14 Apr. 2017. Web. 24 Sept. 2017.

SOURCE NOTES

4. Paul A. Thompson. "J. Cole: *4 Your Eyez Only*." *Pitchfork*. Condé Nast, 14 Dec. 2016. Web. 24 Sept. 2017.

5. Sowmya Krishnamurthy. "J. Cole Contemplates Life & Death on *4 Your Eyez Only*." *Billboard*. Billboard-Hollywood Reporter Media Group, 14 Dec. 2016. Web. 12 Sept. 2017.

6. Paul A. Thompson. "Review: J. Cole *4 Your Eyez Only*." *Pitchfork*. Pitchfork, 14 Dec. 2016. Web. 18 Oct. 2017.

7. J. Cole. "4 Your Eyes Only." *Genius*. Genius Media Group, n.d. Web. 24 Sept. 2017.

8. J. Cole. "Foldin Clothes." *Genius*. Genius Media Group, n.d. Web. 24 Sept. 2017.

9. Jon Caramanica. "J. Cole, the Platinum Rap Dissident, Steps Back from the Spotlight." *New York Times*. New York Times Company, 14 Apr. 2017. Web. 24 Sept. 2017.

10. J. Cole. "She's Mine, Pt. 2." *Genius*. Genius Media Group, n.d. Web. 24 Sept. 2017.

11. "J. Cole Talks *Born Sinner*, Marriage and Acting." *HipHopCanada*. HipHopCanada.com, 16 Oct. 2013. Web. 2 Oct. 2017.

CHAPTER 9. THE MAN AND THE MESSAGE

1. Leonard Moore. "The Coronation of a Hip-Hop Underdog." *PopMatters*. PopMatters.com, 4 Apr. 2017. Web. 12 Sept. 2017.

2. David Smyth. "The Gentle Rapper: J. Cole Interview." *Evening Standard*. Evening Standard, 9 Dec. 2014. Web. 12 Sept. 2017.

3. "J. Cole Talks Rough Childhood on *2014 Forest Hills Drive*." *Music Times*. Music Times, 9 Dec. 2014. Web. 12 Sept. 2017.

4. Sowmya Krishnamurthy. "From St. John's University to Madison Square Garden, J. Cole Comes Home." *Village Voice*. Village Voice, 28 July 2015. Web. 11 Sept. 2017.

5. "5 People Who Love J. Cole, From Jay Z to President Obama." *Billboard*. Billboard-Hollywood Reporter Media Group, 11 Aug. 2016. Web. 12 Sept. 2017.

6. Iyana Robertson. "J. Cole Commemorates *The Warm Up*'s 5-Year Anniversary with an Open Letter." *Vibe*. Billboard-Hollywood Reporter Media Group, 15 June 2014. Web. 11 Sept. 2017.

7. Sowmya Krishnamurthy. "From St. John's University to Madison Square Garden, J. Cole Comes Home." *Village Voice*. Village Voice, 28 July 2015. Web. 11 Sept. 2017.

8. "J. Cole's Greatest Give-Back Moments with Fans." *BET*. BET Interactive, 28 Jan. 2016. Web. 12 Sept. 2017.

9. Rachaell Davis. "ESSENCE Fest Spotlight: Dreamville's Ari Lennox is Exactly Where She Belongs & Thankful for Everything She Went through to Get There." *Essence*. Essence Communications, 3 Mar. 2017. Web. 12 Sept. 2017.

10. "J. Cole's Greatest Give-Back Moments with Fans." *BET*. BET Interactive, 28 Jan. 2016. Web. 12 Sept. 2017.

11. John Kennedy. "You Know the Man behind J. Cole's Dreamville Movement?" *Vibe*. Billboard-Hollywood Reporter Media Group, 10 Dec. 2014. Web. 12 Sept. 2017.

12. "About the Dreamville Foundation." *Dreamville*. Dreamville Foundation, n.d. Web. 12 Sept. 2017.

13. "Road to Homecoming: Episode 1." *HBO*. Home Box Office, Web. n.d. 12 Sept. 2017.

INDEX

From ESP to vampires, Alicia Klepeis loves to research fun and out-of-the-ordinary topics that make nonfiction exciting for readers. Klepeis began her career at the National Geographic Society. She is the author of more than 60 children's books. Her middle grade historical novel *A Time for Change* was released in 2016. She has also written more than 100 articles in magazines, such as *National Geographic Kids*. Alicia is currently working on several projects involving unusual animals, American history, and circus science. She lives with her family in upstate New York. She would love to get the chance to see J. Cole perform live.